T0113597

YOUR DEVIL SELF
VS.
YOUR ANGEL SELF

HARVI VILKS

authorHOUSE®

AuthorHouse™ UK
1663 Liberty Drive
Bloomington, IN 47403 USA
www.authorhouse.co.uk
Phone: UK TFN: 0800 0148641 (Toll Free inside the UK)
        UK Local: 02036 956322 (+44 20 3695 6322 from outside the UK)

© 2021 Harvi Vilks. All rights reserved.

No part of this book may be reproduced, stored in a retrieval system, or
transmitted by any means without the written permission of the author.

Published by AuthorHouse 05/03/2021

ISBN: 978-1-6655-8484-5 (sc)
ISBN: 978-1-6655-8483-8 (e)

Print information available on the last page.

Any people depicted in stock imagery provided by Getty Images are models,
and such images are being used for illustrative purposes only.
Certain stock imagery © Getty Images.

This book is printed on acid-free paper.

Because of the dynamic nature of the Internet, any web addresses or
links contained in this book may have changed since publication and
may no longer be valid. The views expressed in this work are solely those
of the author and do not necessarily reflect the views of the publisher,
and the publisher hereby disclaims any responsibility for them.

This book is dedicated to my brothers who provided me with value before the years of my rediscovery. To Jaspal, who has provided me with guidance and wisdom during my own difficult times; to Gurmit, for providing me the best Christmas present that a kid could ever have; and to Ambrat, for providing me accommodation when I needed it. And to my sister, Jasvinder, who loves reading books.

CONTENTS

YOU VS YOU, EVERY MOMENT OF EVERY SECOND

This book is for people who want to go on a journey to become better versions of themselves by changing their way of thinking—and for those who have a desire to learn more about their true nature. If you are reading this right now, it tells me that you have what it takes to change yourself, as there are no limitations to expanding your mind. But so many people around the world will never change; they are holding on to their limited beliefs, as they have so conditioned themselves that they are starting to believe this is the way they are going to think for the rest of their lives. They have closed their minds and almost shut them off completely to new information. Do not be this person.

If you are in a low vibrational state right now, you may become so used to it on a daily basis that it becomes your normal state of consciousness. When you see other people with similar problems, you will automatically assume that it is OK to be in this condition, and you may not attempt to make a change or even *think* about changing. How many people have you seen in your life who are constantly joyful in the way they feel and in what they do? A few people? A lot of people? These people know that the secret to happiness is knowing how to control your mind.

I hope this book can help you open up your thoughts to greater wisdom and knowledge, whether you are on a road to enlightenment or just want to get rid of negativity in your life. Please read it chapter by chapter; if you skip some parts, you may not understand the message you come across, as there are some parts to this book about philosophy that are not directly about you. You may need to read this book at a slower pace than usual (and over a period of time) because this is how I have intended for it to be read. If you try to read the whole book as quickly as possible, you may miss the entire point of it, and you might not fully benefit from it.

This book will help you in more ways than you know. It is also about others in some ways, as you will come to see. It is your decision how you want to perceive the information in this book. You are in control of your thoughts, not this book. I believe it is a human right for all of us to push ourselves to be our best in all we can possibly do (for positivity purposes, of course, and not the opposite).

You may have already come across and watched videos on how to manifest desires in your life, or self-help tutorials. But when you are putting in too much focus on watching and listening, you might not be putting your attention on the *creation* and *intuition* part of what you are intended to learn. You may also not be following the videos thoroughly with action and intent. This is why most people's lives are stuck in limbo; their minds do not want them to create action, especially for a people who already have minds conditioned for being lazy. These videos may help to some degree, but a majority of the time, they are telling you what needs to happen, yet they do not show you how to make it happen. Some may, but people are sitting there watching and doing nothing else to make that happen.

When a video does tell you what you can expect from it, it is usually to persuade you to pay a premium to join a course which redirects you out of any video content or any other social media. That is where they show you their techniques of how to transform yourself to a better version, but only after you have paid them a large amount of money. I am writing about this so you do not have to pay vast amounts of money in this way. Don't get me wrong—some of these courses may be worth it, but most of them are not. You just have research and find out which ones are the most compatible and of value to you, if you are determined to take that direction.

Moving along from videos and paid online courses, I have written this book in a certain way to be as simple and effective as possible, and hopefully straight to the point. However, I do need you to be fully committed to all the teachings and exercises I am going to be elaborating on because this will tap into your subconscious mind, and you will see life from a different perspective.

If you use your mind correctly (via this book), you will appreciate your own life and others around you a whole lot more than you ever did before. You must have heard the phrase "knowledge is power." But I will tell you: that it is not the case. Knowledge is *not* power. It is the *use* of knowledge that is power, because what is the point of having this kind of knowledge if you are not going to use it properly and in the correct positive manner? That is why I suggest you use the knowledge in this book and turn that into action. And when I say *action*, I am talking about changing your behaviour.

It is very important that you read this book all the way to the end. You will notice subconsciously that every chapter is interconnected, and only at the end will you have a greater awareness of your mind, body, and soul. Have integrity for yourself as well, as this will help you focus.

If you plan to read through this whole book and not go through my methods of teaching and exercises, just let me stop you now. Put this book down, walk away, and carry on being your old self, because simply reading this book is not going to help you change. This may sound harsh, but in order for you to change, I will need your full engagement so you can transform your thinking for the better. There will be times where your old self will tell you to give up and put this book away; remind yourself that this old belief system is not accepted anymore, as it no longer benefits you.

Your old self will try to stop you from becoming a better version of yourself. It will try to persuade you to stay in your comfort zone. This is because it wants to avoid new patterns of behaviour. But have faith in yourself, because there will be a change in you, whether you think that it has happened straight away or not.

Now before I move any further, let me tell you the reason I wanted to write this book. It is simply to provide value to people's lives—*your* life, *this* life. Everyone's life journey is different, and you might think it has similarities to someone else's viewpoints or beliefs, but that is not the case. Everyone receives and perceives information differently, even though you might have learnt or read the same thing. Just like a key to a lock, every door is going to be different for every house. So each person reading this will have different results to the questions they will answer. Yes, I have a few questions for you to answer, but do not worry. They are not difficult, but they are necessary for you to grow.

You have a purpose on earth to fulfil, whether you know it or not. You will know you have fulfilled this purpose when there is a deeper meaning to your existence and you are getting more out of your life. So let's make your life a positive one, and let's take it step by step by using your mind correctly.

I will be using metaphors to get my point across, and I also want to point out that there is no end goal to this rewiring of your thoughts, because the knowledge you have gained will always remain within you. It is your duty to not fall back into your old self again. There will be times when I am subjective and write about myself or other people (only because of life experiences and to give you my personal experiences), but mostly this book is about *you* and for *you*.

The first chapter will start at the very beginning of when you came into this world. Why start there, you may ask? That is a very good question. It is because every moment of your life matters, and this is the very reason why you are where you are right now, at this point in time.

CHAPTER 1

THE CONDITIONING: AN EARLY INDICATION

There is a reason you think the way you do. When we are born, we are born into servitude. By the time we are 6 months old or so, we are already obeying our parents/guardians. Our awareness may have slightly increased, and our motor functions are developing, but we still have no idea what is going on around us. Now this part of the conditioning is vital, because your parents or guardians will create a chain of events making you think or react in a certain way, and this can go in a number of directions depending how they have raised you.

Here is one example: You are 1 year old, and you are sitting in the baby chair, getting spoon-fed by your parents or guardians. The only motor function you are using at that very moment is opening and closing your mouth. You are conditioned to either eat the food or reject it.

Now move on a few years. You are now 3 years old, but your parents or guardians have not changed the way they have fed (conditioned) you. I want you to think about that for a moment.

There is no right or wrong answer in the way parents or guardians would feed and raise their child (unless they have ill intentions). But like I said before, every person is conditioned to think in a certain way. Let's revert back to when you were 1 year old again.

Imagine you are sitting in the baby chair, but this time, instead of getting spoon-fed by your parents or guardians, you have been given some food that you can hold in your own hand to eat by yourself. Again, this goes on for a couple of years, until you are the 3 years old. What do you think the differences would be between the two conditions?

The difference is that as the first baby, you are on autopilot and not really thinking for yourself, as your parents or guardians are doing the thinking for you. You will be too dependent on them when growing up. As the second baby, you are thinking outside the box. Not only you are holding your own food, you are feeding yourself as well. You will even know how much to bite off or chew automatically.

The same principle applies when you are starting school. Imagine you did not attend nursery or year reception and jumped straight into year one. However, your peers in your age group attended pre-year one. Most of them are going to be more confident than you, because they are used to seeing teachers and other children around them. Their personal development will occur more quickly than yours. Meanwhile, you are experiencing school for the first time, so you will maybe be at the opposite end of confidence.

This is the cause and effect that has already been implanted in your brain. At this age, you will not even realise it is happening, but it is. If this did happen to you, you were likely to be in the category of a shy, introverted person if you skipped pre-year one.

But do not take my word for it. While you are growing up, this all can change and go in a different direction. You can either finish school and graduate full of confidence, happiness, and enjoyment, or you can finish school and graduate with misery, distress, and low self-esteem. This all depends on your conditioning. Every single decision you have ever made in your past is a direct cause of what you are now. There may be times when other people (like your parents, for example) made choices for you, directly or indirectly, but for the most part, it was always you.

Speaking of school, you are also being conditioned to study hard. Teachers and parents/guardians will encourage you to study hard because that is the way they studied when they were at school. It is obvious they are going to condition their students the same way. No teacher or parent/guardian will tell a student to study blissfully, study happily, or study joyfully, because they think studying hard will put pressure on your head—and putting pressure on your head equals better success and top marks on your exams. Yet whichever way teachers lecture you, you will get the same desired results if you study happily, joyfully, or blissfully, but without the stress in your head.

The choices you make every single day of your life predominantly control who you are. I will elaborate more on this, but before I do, I would like to go over this exercise with you, because you need to know exactly where you stand at this point in time. Remember that I need you to put the effort in. All of this is relevant for all the chapters ahead. Please pay attention and participate, as this is only for your benefit.

Exercise Part 1

Find a pen and paper. I want you to jump back into memory lane. I need you to put on your thinking cap and recall a time when you were in your youth and felt a powerful emotion that you still remember today (whether good or bad, happy or sad). I want you to close your eyes and imagine yourself back then in those moments. Connect with them and feel what you went through. What do you see? Who is there? What is happening?

Do this exercise now, before you read any further. Sit down somewhere or lie on a bed if you need to. Try to relax and spend a few minutes with your eyes closed. It is best to make sure you are undisturbed.

Now I am going to ask some questions, and I want you to write down your answers. Your answers can be short or long, blunt or vague or specific—it does not matter as long as you write something. Do not worry if you cannot think of the answer right now. This is not a test. Deep down, you will know the answer.

Be honest with yourself when you write down your answers. Take as long as you need to; there is no time limit. When you are ready, the questions are as follows:

1. How did you *feel* about yourself growing up during your teenage years or younger, and why did you feel this way?
2. What did your peers at school think of you, and why did they treat and think of you in this sort of way?
3. What do you think your personality was like back then? Were you a confident person or a shy person when you were younger? And why was that?
4. What were your relationships like with your brother, sister, mother, father, and other family members? Who did you get along with or not get along with, and why was this the case?

Take your time with this before you keep reading.

Exercise Part 2

Once you've answered all of the questions in part 1, take a quick break if you have to and then come back for the next set of questions. I want you to look in the mirror (do this now at this very moment). Look deep into your own eyes for a minute or two. When you've done that part, come back to this book.

When that person was staring back at you, what emotion did you feel? Happiness? Resentment? Sadness? Joy? Guilt? Whatever the case, please answer the following questions. Remember to be truthful to yourself, as there is no right or wrong answer. Just take your time as before.

5. At this very moment, how do you feel about yourself now, and why do you feel this way? What is the root cause for you to feel this way?
6. At this present moment, what do people around you think of you (when you are at a place of work, home, etc)? Why do you think they act this way towards you?
7. What is your personality like now? Has it changed over the years, and why is that?
8. What are your relationships like now with your siblings, parents, or partner/spouse? Or are you lonely? What is root cause of this?
9. What is your physical health like on a scale of 1 to 10—1 being very poor and 10 being very good? Why did you choose that number?

Take a quick break if you need to. I hope you have answered all of these questions before you move on to the next chapter (it will all makes sense in the later topics).

I have presented these questions for a very specific reason. If you did answer all of them, it shows your true self, that you have the willpower to make a change in your current situation. You want change for the better, right? We all do. But most people decide not to because they are afraid of stepping out of their comfort zone. *Do not let this be you.*

Dualism plays a vital role in your life, more than you may know (I will explain a little more about dualism in the latter parts of this book). But it's like this: A devil and an angel are sitting on your shoulders, on opposite sides. They are constantly sending you thoughts throughout your life, every second, every moment of every day. The question to you is, which one do you listen to the most? And another question to you is, who is actually the good and who is actually the bad between the pair? You already know the answer to this question, because whichever way you perceive it, it resonates inside you.

But let's just say for the purpose of this book that the devil is bad and the angel is good. The survival brain will be telling you it is safer and easier to do exactly the same thing you did yesterday and the previous day and the days before that. It wants you to repeat and reoccur, because that feels so familiar that it wants you to do that again and again. I am not saying this way of life is wrong; what I am saying is, this way of life is not making you expand. There is a better way.

When you finally realise that you do want a better way of life by telling your old self that enough is enough, you will need to make a change in your circumstances. The survival brain will already be firing signals at you to stay in your comfort zone. How many times have you tried to stop doing something or to do something new but fail or procrastinate because you lack the intent—for example, going to the gym or trying to give up on drugs and alcohol. Your mind may be unbalanced, and it is time to fix it.

There are ways to break out of this cycle. Carry on reading this book. You need patience in order to do this. If you rush things and start skipping parts, you will have missed the point, and your old self will be getting the better of you.

You need to know that some of these are cravings that have a very low vibrational state of energy, and they are making you very guilt-ridden or lazy. There is a way to replace them; you have the power to control this, because you are in the control room, and you get to decide to listen more to the angel side of your subconscious that can unleash your inner creativity and intuition. Once you are more in line with this side, you will rebalance your mind, and you can move your cravings in a different direction, such as being excited to learn new things every day or to become more active in your work life or home life. It will not feel like you have a dire or dreaded life anymore (if it already feels that way). Your approach to life will change for the better, because your mind will feel more industrious to any obstacles that intersect with you on a daily basis.

Over the following chapters, we are going to go into more depth on the questions that you have answered. It's all connected within you, as you will see. If you are feeling low right now, hopefully this next chapter will guide you in the healing process. Like I said before, have faith in yourself. Trust your heart.

PART 1

YOUR HEALTH IS YOUR WEALTH

CHAPTER 2

DEPRESSION AND FEELING LOW

This is one of the topics I pondered writing about in this book, because if you are in a depressed or low vibrational state, chances are that reading this book is the last thing on your mind right now. But I know you may want to be healed from this trauma, and I want you to be. Even if you are mentally well right now, it is still worth reading this chapter, as it will make you see the mind from a different perspective.

You may or may not feel mentally well right now, or you probably have come across someone who has suffered depression. You have a duty to help yourself or others (if you are in this position), and I will show you how to redirect your thoughts by rewiring your conscious and subconscious mind.

Depression is a silent illness and can be triggered at any time in a person's life. Depression does not care what you look like, what religious beliefs you hold, how much money you have, or what relationship status you have. You cannot know if people have these symptoms just by looking at them, as sometimes you can misinterpret others' body language by thinking they have stress when they might not. A depressed person will also have a lack of concentration and a lack of focus, as the mind has been hacked, like a computer with a virus.

If you are in this position and feel depressed, there is good news: an end to your pain. I know it may not feel this way right now, but trust me, this will eventually pass. I know because I also suffered depression for a long, *long* time, so I know it is not a good feeling.

Everyone reacts differently to depression. For you to gradually improve your health, you need to know how your mind works. But first, have you ever heard of the word *stoicism?* It means training oneself not to show any emotional baggage if anything bad happens, regardless of the event or situation. This is what it is all about—controlling your mind, using it correctly and healthily, by getting rid of all the clutter that is already in your head. The next paragraph is a great metaphor for your mind, body, and soul, so please pay attention if you are in a low-self-esteem state of consciousness.

Your body is like one big computer. Your heart is like your battery supply: if you switch it off, you will die. Your immune system is like your antivirus: if you did not have it, you would constantly be sick. And your brain is like your internal memory card: without it, you will not operate. What has happened is some parts of your central processing unit (the CPU of your brain) have been corrupted with malicious content. And what you need to do is *update* your old computer software programme (which is your past belief) in your brain to wipe it out.

It's like this: whenever you get injured physically, your body will need time to heal. This is exactly the same for your brain. Your brain is like an antenna that receives and transmits constant information, whether consciously, subconsciously, or unconsciously. Your brain needs time to heal. At this very minute, it is automatically getting rebooted, as your old software is getting updated because some parts are no longer required. But you have no idea that this is happening, because you may think you feel no change in your current situation.

Let me acknowledge that a change for the good is happening, even though right now it may not feel this way, as it's processing behind the scenes of your subconscious mind. It is replacing your corrupt data and redirecting it into cached files where it is not needed. Depending on each person, this rebooting process can take as long as it has to. So stop worrying. A positive outcome will come your way. Remember to trust in time, as it will take a little while.

You may feel sometimes that it is getting worse by the days or weeks, but know this: for you to get better, you need to beat the peak of this depression. You have to leave your ego and pride behind, because there is so much clutter in your mind right that it is clogging up your head space. You need to do this by letting go of your past emotions that no longer serve your current situation. You will come out stronger mentally than you were before. Remember, though, that your old thoughts will always remain in the deleted cache folder, and there is no need for you to restore them. Keep them at bay.

Make use of the tools provided for you, such as helplines and going to your GP. You need to encourage yourself and just get up and search for them. Two other main things are to stop watching films that are depressing and stop listening to sad music that is also depressing, as these are only going to increase the mental pressure in your head. Instead, do the opposite. If that helps, start listening to happy music and stop watching negative TV news and reading newspapers, as they are full of negativity.

Also, do not skip going to the doctor, as doctors will serve your best interest. If you need to take antidepressants, just take them. Do not fear what other people will think of you. Do not worry what friends and family think of you as they try to help you. Remember that your doctor is not there to judge you either. Doctors are there to help you as much as possible. But the longer you avoid visiting your doctor, the worse it can get for you. So pick yourself up, make that appointment, and visit your doctor. Accepting that you need help is the first move toward getting better. So accept it and make that move.

Has there ever been a time when you avoided going to the doctor because you assumed if you went, there might be some bad news coming your way? But when you finally did go with your gut instincts and courage, and when your doctor tested you, a few days later, your test results came in and the doctor said you were completely fine? You then realised you were worrying for no apparent reason about a future that never happened.

Remember, this is your survival brain stopping you from moving forward because it makes up stories in your head to stop you from leaving this grey area. Push yourself up and do the right thing and go, because if you don't, you never will. Now is the time to take a stand and stop making excuses. Your survival brain is making you think this way. This kind of behaviour has led you nowhere except around in circles, hasn't it?

Rewire your mind. Try reprogramming your brain. Whenever an ill thought pops up (which will probably happen quite often), just keep reminding yourself that these old behaviour patterns no longer serve your future self.

Every time an ill thought pops up, quickly acknowledge that it is happening and reaffirm to yourself that you have the power to control these thoughts. You are holding on to the lever in your brain, and only you can change the level of your emotions by turning it down. Think as if this corrupt data in your brain is just getting analysed every time this ill thought pattern pops up.

Remember, it is the way you are living right now that is causing you to feel this way. So even changing the way you are currently living can have an impact on your behaviour. You can start by exercising occasionally, as this has a proven effect on your low vibration. You can also change this low mood by eating and drinking healthily and thinking robustly. And you need a big shift in your conscious and subconscious mind right now, as you will soon come to read.

So retell your current self that these old behaviour patterns no longer serve your future self. Say the words out loud. I recommend doing so because it helps you heal faster. Say them now.

From time to time, you may feel that things are getting worse, but try to avert your mind by focusing on any good emotions you have experienced over the years of your life. If these ill thoughts keeps popping up, try to focus on the positive activities you have done in the past and think about interests and hobbies you have enjoyed. Try to tap into those good emotions as if you were there at this present moment in time.

As you may know what the root cause is of this depressed feeling, try not to look at it in a negative way. Instead, alternate it and look at it from a positive perspective. I will give you one example of a random person whose partner left, and this caused a feeling of sadness. So what is the positivity of this outcome? This individual is now free to do as he or she pleases and does not need to see the ex-partner as a burden anymore. In fact, this individual is better off without the ex-partner.

Whatever situation has made you feel depressed or low, search for a positive outcome from it, even though that may seem difficult to do. There will always be at least one if you focus. Do not constantly think on the negative. Take your time and think on at least one positive instead. One quick example is people dying young with their whole life ahead of them. It is hard to lose someone so young, but know that the individual is not in pain anymore. Do not make yourself suffer.

The other thing I want you to take on board before I finish this the part of this topic is to have patience. It will feel difficult, but give your mind the time it needs to heal. Your new future self is rebooting, and once that is over—because it will be—these ill thoughts will become part of the distant past, and you will become a stronger person (mentally speaking) than you ever were before. You may not feel this way right now, but one day you will look back at it and say *I beat this*.

If you have gotten this far by reading everything, I want to say congratulations, because the biggest secret to everything is *choice*. And when I say everything, I mean *everything*:

- You have a choice as to how you want to feel right now.
- You have a choice as to how you want to view others.
- You have a choice as to whether you want be lazy or active.
- You have a choice as to whether to read this book or not.
- You have a choice as to whether you want to be shy or confident.

Choice after choice. Master this skill, and you can overcome obstacles with ease—mentally speaking, of course. Yes, you read that correctly: choosing how you feel is a skill for your mind. The reason I did not mention this earlier is because I needed to know if you had what it takes to get this far.

If you are feeling low right now or guilty or whatever, that is also by choice. You chose to feel this way, and you can choose to un-feel this way. And that choice was always yours. So any feeling that you do not want, choose any other emotion that you do want.

Now that you are at the end of this chapter, it is vital for you to continue reading this book, because you will only get stronger mentally. Have trust in yourself. You have what it takes to be your better self.

Your life matters. This is your wake-up call. Master the skill of choice!

CHAPTER 3

EAT TO LIVE, NOT LIVE TO EAT

Moving away from your mind, your body mass index is determined by the foods and liquids you consume (unless it's by a medical condition) and how much exercise you do. If throughout most of your life you have been eating junk food on a regular basis, and then one day you decide you have had enough of this way of eating and you want to start eating more healthily, immediately your survival brain will jump into action and try its best to put you back to square one. You may buy healthy foods like vegetables or fruits, but your survival brain will send you many signals that burgers and fries are tasty, less expensive, and mostly fulfilling.

If you are already at the level where you are eating healthily on a regular basis, that is a positive and well done you. Keep it up and do not change this habit. However, if you are not there yet and you try to make a change, your survival brain will be forcing you not to; it wants you to stay the way you are, as a fraction of what you really could be. If this has already happened to you, it is going to be very challenging to change. But only you have the power, because you control your choices. Control your mind and do not let your mind control you. Remember, it is your old self versus your new transformed self and nobody else.

This an important factor in your life right now. Once you go with intent, you need to carry on eating healthily with intent, because if you do not, your physical health will deteriorate. Here is a quick examination for you to do. The next time you decide to eat heavy junk food, like greasy burgers and fries, notice your heartbeat. Focus on the beating while you are eating, and you will notice that your heart is feeling heavier. That is because your blood pressure is getting higher, as it needs to work harder. That is not a good sign for you, is it?

In order to move away from this and break that barrier to eating healthily, you will need a shift in your consciousness. Just imagine you decided with intent to start eating healthy foods for x amount of weeks. On any one of those days, your survival brain will be there sending you subtle thoughts to procrastinate or just give up. If it succeeds, you have failed. You will be back to your old self again, wondering where it all went wrong. I can only guide you and show you the way. You have to put the rest of the effort in yourself.

If you are already eating in a healthy way, well done you. If you are not, you are already in a position where you can actually make a difference in your eating habits. You may be eating these genetically modified unhealthy processed meats, and your conscious mind knows it is wrong for your health, but your survival brain has put this thought at the back of your mind by making you not even have the thought to change in the first place. But you do know the importance of changing your habits, right? Once you have this thought to change, your survival brain kicks into action, persuading you that you are doing fine just the way you are.

Let me be clear to you: *No*, you are *not* doing fine the way you are right now. This old thinking is clogging up your arteries, and your heart needs to pump blood twice as hard as it should. Your survival brain will hold you back by making you think that you are still very young and eating like this will not hurt. And this is the part where it traps you. If you say you will start eating healthily tomorrow or next week, the survival brain is making you think this way, because that is your conditioned way of thinking. You are most likely not to change, because if you had this state mentally right now, you would not be thinking of changing your eating habits tomorrow or next week. You would be acting on it to change as soon as possible—that is if you avoided listening to your survival brain and went with intent. I suggest you do this. Change your intentions.

The survival brain is a trap for your way of thinking, because when you do say "I am going to start eating healthily tomorrow or next week," when the time comes, you may have already decided that you cannot be bothered. Your survival brain has beaten you again. And before you know it, years may have gone by, and you will only have yourself to blame, as it is nobody else's fault.

Do not make excuses for yourself. You have made excuse after excuse and blamed other things, people, places, or events in your life, as it is easy for your survival brain to stay inactive. It is time to stop making these lousy excuses and change your behaviour, as it has kept you from being your better self. It is now time for you to live longer, so do the right thing and make that change as soon as possible. Imagine yourself in a couple of years' time looking much much healthier physically and mentally. To get there, you need to act now. It is now or never. You have that choice.

Even though you might appear healthy on the outside, your guts will give you a completely different diagnosis. I would like to go over an exercise with you. The first step is *acceptance* that you want to make that change of your current conditioned self. This is an important step for you to make, as you need to step out of your comfort zone. Only then can you make a difference in your health.

You will need to start putting your mind on focus mode every time you think of food in order to start eating healthily. Think of healthy food instead of junk food if you find this hard. Your cravings for junk food will pop up from time to time (remember, this feeling of craving is a choice), but always remind your survival brain that if junk food can pop up for no reason, so can healthy food. Try to redirect your thoughts. You are better than your old self. You can do this!

Exercise Part 1

Here is something you can do right now. Get a pen and paper, go to your kitchen or food storage, and make a list of all the unhealthy food you have on one side and all the healthy food you have on the other side. If you have more unhealthy food stored in your house than healthy food, you need to ask yourself why that is and how can you change it. Get rid of food that is not beneficial for you and your family in the long run. Remember, your health is your wealth.

Do not get me wrong. I am not asking you to get rid of all the junk food in your house. What I am asking you to do is rebalance your food intake. For example, start eating more on the healthy side. Week by week, try to increase your healthy food intake while decreasing your junk food intake. Gradually, over time, you will start to eat more healthily. But this is a process you have to carry on and go after with intent, because your old habits can quickly sneak back up.

Do not push your partner or family members to change their eating habits, as this can cause conflicts. Do not forget that this book is for *you*, not them. Separate your food consumption from theirs if you have to. If they are willing to make that change, they will. You can encourage them by your persuasive actions and by making them understand the importance of changing, but they have to make their own choice, as you cannot think for them.

Moving away from that, the question for you is, what kind of health do you want for you and your family? The mediocre health that you all are struggling with? Do you feel sluggish and tired most of the time? That is because of your eating habits. Remember, you have put yourself in this way, and you can get yourself out. Have trust in yourself to do the right thing for you and your family.

Make that change now! Not tomorrow, not next week—*now*!

Exercise Part 2

This is another way for you to rewire your subconscious mind. I will need you to do the following action. I understand it may feel uncomfortable at first, but your subconscious mind will get used to it. And it is best for you to be alone and undisturbed, if that helps.

> Look at your old self in the mirror and say the following:
>
> "Hello, [your name]. Your old eating habits no longer serve my true self. From now on, I am going to start eating healthier, and I will continue to do so."

Your survival brain will try to put you off saying these words out loud, because someone may be close by who sees or hears you. The first thing people will do is ridicule you, and this might put you off more than before. This could stop you from taking action, but do not let it. Incentivise yourself.

It may feel odd, weird, or bizarre to talk to yourself out loud, but the more you do it, the more you will get used to hearing your own voice. Every day when you wake up and start your morning routine, start chanting those words. Do not let your survival brain put you off. You can do this. I have faith in you to change.

It is very important not to lie to yourself. Be a person of your word, because this is the part where you need to stay committed and focused. You will need to say that phrase every morning for at least one month while making sure you eat healthily. Download a free nutritious health sheet (if that helps) from the internet if you need to. It will help you set a timetable of which foods to eat and when. Foods with lots of fibre and protein are good for your body. But remember, if you have allergy issues, it is always best to talk to your GP first. The GP will also help you for your best interest.

During this transformation, if you are bloating and constipated, this should reduce gradually. One important piece of advice for you is to be aware of your survival brain, because you will be tempted by friends or family offering you unhealthy snacks such as sweets and chocolates. Still, most friends and family will be proud of you for making this change.

But be cautious, as there may be one or two people you need to be aware of, as they may ridicule you and put you off by saying it will not last. They may say this because they cannot do what you can, as they have their own insecurities. Just prove them wrong by carrying on eating healthily with intent and remind your true self every day that "I am stronger than yesterday. I can handle these cravings with ease, as I am in control of these thoughts, and I am better than this."

CHAPTER 4

LET US DRINK SOME

Aside from eating healthy foods, there is one thing that people are not doing enough, and that is drinking water. You may feel you are drinking enough water, as sometimes your mind might make you think you are; but in fact, your body does not. Do not chug sugar-infested drinks; they are doing you more harm than good. The people who are selling you these unhealthy drinks are only there to make a profit; they do not care about your health. The only person who can properly look after your own health is you. You may get help from other people, but you still have to take the first step in helping yourself.

You may be drinking these unhealthy sugar drinks as an alternative to water because you think water is making you go to the toilet more often than usual. It is a good sign for your health if you are, because water flushes out of your system far more quickly than any other liquid. In reality, we as humans should not be drinking man-made substances in the first place, unless of course it is medicine or some liquid to enhance your health. But because of the way you were conditioned by yourself, by people, by places, and even by advertisements that you come across, you are on autopilot and consume these unnecessary products. Let's put a stop to this right now.

I saw so many propaganda advertisements back in the day that said if you consume this energy drink, you can run and perform 30 per cent better than normal. It is a lie, because it has not been tested and proven. So many people watch this advert, and they believe every word of it. No wonder so many people around the world have health issues.

There is a famous quote from Mark Twain: "It is easier to fool someone than to convince them that they have actually been fooled." These companies have been fooling people for years. So be smart about it and do not drink these drinks.

Back to drinking water: Many people do not drink water enough or hardly any at all. There are a number of reasons why they do not, but one of the main reasons is that it gets in the way of their day-to-day activities, and they cannot be bothered to go so often to the toilet. But that is just an excuse your survival brain has created. It is not good for your health, and it is time to change that.

Imagine that you are doing an eight-hour shift at work, and you are working under pressure, afraid of not hitting your targets. You might fear that if you drink too much water, it will send you to the toilet many times over, and you do not want to get told off by the supervisor or boss. Let me tell you, you can go to the toilet as many times you like; they cannot stop you from going. That is a human right. But if you are worried that you won't hit your targets, you will if you start working smarter.

One important thing to remember is, if you carry on drinking water with intent, your body will get used to it, and eventually you will not have go to the toilet as often as you did. But if you are in an area where it is difficult to leave your position, then space out your drinking. Have one small sip from a bottle of water every fifteen minutes or so, or whatever drinking habits suit you best in your situation. But you *must* drink water regularly. If you are challenged by your boss or supervisor, then challenge them back. Ask why they are allowed to have a drink next to *their* desk.

Remember, you can always find solutions to problems if you work things out in a civilised manner. If you cannot have a water bottle next to you, there should be some drink fountains or water basins adjacent to where you work. Drinking water is a human right and is mandatory in a work environment. Like I have mentioned before, be smart about it. Your health will suffer if you do not drink enough water. If you follow this procedure, you should have no excuse.

Drinking water when you wake up is a must in the morning and beneficial for your body too. Try to drink some warm to hot water every morning, and let it settle there for at least half an hour before you start to eat your breakfast. Also, drink some warm to hot water just before you are about to sleep. This will also help your digestion run smoothly.

The thing for you to note is the importance of drinking water and eating healthily every day. You will not only improve your gut problems (if you have any), you will feel you have more energy than ever before. No more feelings of sluggishness and fatigue. Remember, the key to succeeding is to change your conditioning. If you change your old self, you can change your end result.

It is all just a matter of choice, because the power is already within you. You just have to become your future self as soon as possible. The time to change is now.

CHAPTER 5

PHYSICAL ENDURANCE

If you recall, previously I asked you a specific question about your physical health on a scale of 1 to 10. If you do not execute any physical exercises while eating healthily on a regular basis, your score should be below average. Yes, below average. If you have scored yourself over 7, you are overestimating. You may think you are healthy because your conditioned mind tells you this, but in reality, you are not.

You may go to a place of work where you are required to do physical labour, but that is not making you physically healthy. In fact, it is making you descend to a lower level of health. Your survival brain is making you think you are OK. Just because you are moving your body around by the nature of your work does not mean that you are in a healthy state of well-being.

I can understand that some readers might have a physical illness that is stopping them from getting healthy, but think to yourself, is there an alternative way for you to getting physically healthy? Ask yourself the right question. Instead of thinking negatively or saying *I cannot do this*, ask yourself *How can I do this?* Or *What can I do to make myself more physically healthy?* Once you find the answer, then ask yourself afterwards, *Why am I not following this through?*

For other readers, I say you definitely have no excuse for not doing any exercise at all. We all live busy lifestyles, but that is not an excuse for you to sit on your sofa or bed right now. We all have spare time in our day-to-day life. In one day, there are twenty-four hours, so let us see this through from a random person's perspective.

The average time to sleep is eight hours. You may go to work (including travelling there and back) for approximately ten hours on average a day, depending on the country you live in. From here, you still have six hours left. Within that time, you start going about your business on a day-to-day routine. Maybe you start watching nonsense TV or constantly consume technology, such as gadgets, smartphones, browsing on the internet, going on social sites, and watching videos on social media on a regular basis. You have plenty of time to exercise, so stop with the excuses.

Maybe you have a dog, and you need to take it for a walk. Or maybe you are looking after your children, and you need to make them dinner. Or just maybe you have other things to attend to. Whatever it is, you can still make time for yourself. So stop putting too much emphasis on other situations, because you need self-time as well.

There is a time and a space for everything. If you are in a situation where you are thinking there is never enough time, that is because you are not using your time efficiently. There is enough time, but you are not using the time provided for you correctly. If you really do not have enough time in your day-to-day routine, then something is not right there, and you need to change this pattern.

I can understand you have to spend some time with your animals or children. But you may have conditioned yourself too much, to the point where you think of others far more often than you think of yourself. I also truly understand that you have a duty and responsibility to look after and care for someone or something. But you have a duty and responsibility to look after yourself physically and mentally as well. In order to step out of this box, you first need to accept that you want to change, and only then you can change your routine. You need to know the importance of the value of yourself.

To tap out of this loop that you have created, start thinking smartly. First of all, condition your behaviour to move out of your comfort zone. Remember, this is the biggest step, for you to shift out of your old thinking. If you do not make that choice to change, you are stuck in an infinite loop.

If you have none of the responsibilities mentioned here, then you are simply lazy. Sorry to say this; do not be offended, as this is the truth. Being lazy is a *choice*. Far too many people wake up in the morning and lay in bed daydreaming, yet they are far from acting upon their dreams. I cannot adequately emphasise the importance of your health just by words alone. You need to tap yourself out of this conditioning you have created.

Make that choice. This old behaviour needs to go.

If you have a dog, you have no excuse to avoid exercising. Use your dog to your advantage. Instead of walking your dog, jog with your dog. If you jog for just one minute for the first day, that is OK. Gradually, each day, keep increasing the time. When you do this consistently, your health will improve.

Find a suitable area such as a park or safe path for you and your dog. Do not feel paranoid if you think people are watching you. Even if they *are* watching you, who cares? You are going about your own business, and they are going about theirs. It is mind over matter. But if you still feel uncomfortable, join a gym if you have not already or buy a treadmill and make some space for it in your home or garage. Sitting constantly on your backside is not going to help you.

Remember, it is about your time, and as I have mentioned before, you need to realise how much value you are to your own life. Do not lie to yourself by saying *I am busy* or *I am tired*, because you are not busy or tired. That is your survival brain saying those things. It is time for you to stop making excuse after excuse. Condition your mind now; make that happen and get off your sluggish side.

Use your time properly every day, and you will notice there should be hardly any gaps where time is being wasted. Make an action plan and set goals for your exercise. This way, you know that at this certain time, you are going to exercise each day. Start making this a regular habit.

If you are a person who is looking after children, what is your excuse? You have a TV. Use that to your advantage. Be smart about it, and start watching exercise tutorials instead of garbage. Use your own home as a facility to exercise. Another option is to tell your partner (if you have one) to look after the children while you exercise outside or at home. There are other ways as well; you just need to try harder.

It is time to put those excuses behind you. You just need to get up and act; if you do not, you are just being lazy, and you chose to be this way. If you are feeling lazy, you can also choose not to feel that way. It is all about choice. It always was.

Having an excuse is a choice you have made, and so is a feeling of being energetic. So which one are you going to choose? Are you going to listen to your old self who serves little purpose in your life, or are you going to listen to your true authentic self and have better health in your life?

CHAPTER 6

BECOMING THE STOIC

Death is a natural part of life; that is inevitable. We are all going to face someone who is close to us leaving this world, either peacefully or traumatically, at any time during our lifetime. It does not matter what age they are—whether less than 1 day old or 100 years old. When their time is up, it is up to you how you deal with this. You can either cry and end up in a bad place, or you can accept the situation and carry on with your own life. A majority of people live with too many emotions, and that can lead to mental instability.

War veterans coming back from their service could have post-traumatic stress disorder from seeing horrible scenes of death, violence, and any other malicious situation. I am using this as an example because anyone, anywhere around the world, can have feelings of discomfort. It is about shutting down the part of the brain where emotion resides within you. Whatever situation you are in right now, know that every situation you come across is *neutral* (there is no good, there is no bad), and it will only change when you choose an emotion.

Let me talk about a controversial subject. When the World Trade Centres were hit by the planes, there were two main emotions throughout the world between East and West. Since I am born in the UK, my emotions were residing with the West. The West was devastated, while the East was more or less celebrating. The East and West saw exactly the same thing, but they reacted differently to that situation.

The West mostly thinks the East is a problem, and the East mostly think the West is a problem. But this is the problem the whole world has with propaganda media. There are always going to be wars. This is inevitable because of the way the world system is run. But it does not have to be this way, though this is a whole other subject which I will not discuss because this book is not intended for that.

My point is that people are bringing in too much emotional attachment from ego—who you can or cannot control, who you can or cannot dictate to, what you can and cannot say, what you can or cannot wear, who you can or cannot speak to, etc. Here you can contain the health of your mind by not overthinking. Excessive thinking can lead to your downfall and turmoil.

In order to become the stoic, you must look at your own life as neutral as possible, free from jealousy, free from comparing your life with others, free from attachment, free from feeling emotions. If there is anything you do not like in your life, you can change it. If you cannot change it or work things out, then you must accept it and move on with a neutral emotion.

Even if, for example, you are no longer on speaking terms with a friend or family member—they may have upset you or vice versa—you can forgive them (or forgive yourself) and move on. This does not necessarily mean you have to meet them face-to-face and forgive them. No, quite the opposite. You can forgive them or yourself your own way, because if you are holding on with too much anger, you are still emotionally attached to that person, even if they hate you or you hate them. So let go of this emotion of hate, as it is creating a prison for your mind. Free your mind.

Let's go over a simple common scenario of a problematic person. This person was walking barefooted at home, and while walking, accidentally hit a toe on the corner of a door. This caused a lot of pain in the toe, which resulted in the person kicking the door repeatedly, almost to the point where the door came off its hinges. Later on that day, this person decided to go shopping with the kids. As the family arrived at the parking lot of the store, they were just about to park in a children's designated area when suddenly, a car pulled up and parked in that place, driven by someone who had no children along for the ride. The person we've been following quickly blasted the horn, claiming ownership of the space. This caused a heated argument.

Our problematic person was already having issues way before hitting a toe on the door. The door was not the issue; it did not move in the person's way. The door had always been there. But the person decided to take out some anger on it, as if it was the door's fault. And when it came to the ignorant driver in the parking lot who took the child parking spot, this individual may have parked there purposely because it was a free space. The two drivers shouting abuse at each other was not going to resolve the problem. In fact, it might have made things worse.

Stoic people in this situation would not have blamed the door for accidentally hurting their toes. They would accept it, as it was their own mistake, and they would move on without causing any anger and frustration at people or objects. At the parking lot, a stoic would just ask politely for the person to move the car. A reasonable driver would usually drive away without any negativity. But if that individual did not move, stoics would just find another parking space, as it is beyond their control to move the ignorant driver without feeling angry over it.

This is just a simple example. You may have come across many situations where you have been annoyed, stressed, anxious, etc. But *you* can decide today that these are just emotions of choice that do not need to reside within *you*.

Why do you choose to hold on to negative emotions such as fear, anxiety, stress, worry, and depression? This has not done you any favours, has it? When did you decide to be this kind of person? It is time to choose something better.

PART 2

SELF-RESPECT

CHAPTER 7

CHOICES

To bring out your true self, you need to understand all the choices you have ever made in your past. And I literally mean *all* the choices you have ever made. In fact, I will show you an example of a random person, and we will analyse the choices that person has made:

This person gets up in the morning, goes to work, comes home, has dinner, and goes to sleep—then repeats these steps the following morning. See if you can analyse this and count how many choices the person makes just in the morning routine. I will go through it with you. Remember, this is just an example of one person. Your morning routine could be different.

This person—we'll call him Joe—wakes up at the same time every morning at six o'clock by his alarm clock. He presses the snooze button and stays lying in bed for another fifteen minutes. He looks at the time again and decides to get up and go to the washroom to freshen up. He brushes his teeth, washes his face, goes downstairs, and starts to boil the kettle. After drinking tea or coffee and eating breakfast, he goes back upstairs to change from his pyjamas to his work uniform. He goes back to the washroom to groom his hair. He then goes back downstairs and spends over half an hour on social media on his phone. He looks at the time and gets ready to leave the house. He then sits in his car and prepares to drive to his place of work.

Now, how many choices do you see Joe making in the morning only? There are at least twenty choices and decisions made there alone. Waking up at six o'clock is a decision; waking up by your alarm clock is a decision; pressing the snooze button is another decision; staying in bed daydreaming for another fifteen minutes is another decision; finally getting up out of bed is another decision. Decision after decision. Do you see it now, how many choices Joe has made but does not realise it, as he is on autopilot?

And this is where you are in your own life. You may not realise how many choices, decisions, and actions you have made throughout your whole life because your old self is on autopilot. This is how you are conditioning your mind, because you are repeating the same choices day after day, and you are starting to think this is who you are going to be for the rest of your life. But it does not have to be this way. You can rewire your brain to think and act differently, and there is a proven method.

When you wake up in the morning, get up straight away. Some people remain in bed, lying there daydreaming. When you daydream (even for a few minutes), at that very moment, you are being lazy. You are not becoming the *doer* but instead are becoming the *thinker*. A thinker will only think, while a doer will not only think but get up straight away and *act* with intent.

When a decision has to be made, it may feel uncomfortable, because the survival brain is getting challenged. One thing to remember is that when you make a choice of how you want to feel regardless of any situation—for example, you had a feeling of sadness because you had a flat tyre on your car—you can unmake that feeling of sadness by changing your perspective of how you want to see it or feel it. The choice is yours—whatever emotion you want to feel. Nobody is forcing anyone to feel this discomfort, but you decided to react this way because you think it is normal to do so, and so you do.

This is how you can rewire your old patterns of behaviour— by choosing a better and more efficient one instead of one that is going to cause you annoyance and misery. You can choose the one that is more beneficial to yourself in any situation. Once you have mastered this thought of *choice*, you will be able to unleash the better version of yourself, as you will be able to handle stress and pressure in a calm manner.

Now, let your future self come to life. Your old self has served its purpose.

CHAPTER 8

SELF-LOVE IS NOT NARCISSISM

There are other ways to enhance yourself, such as changing the way you appear to yourself and others. The way you look at yourself will be different from the way people look at you. You may think and say you care or do not care what other people think of you. However, if someone says bad things about you, you are more likely to feel upset about it. When you do feel bad, you start to bring in this emotional attachment with it. The key to this is to detach your mind from other people's opinions, because every person has a right to an opinion, whether good or bad, and you just need to make sure that it does not affect you in any way.

No matter how much you try to please others, they will judge you however they want to. Cynical minds see problems everywhere, as they have conditioned themselves that way. It is pointless to try to change them or make them understand, because they will always go back to their cynical ways— unless they want to see differently, of course. There is no need for you to have sleepless nights just because someone said something upsetting about you.

But if someone directly taunts or insults you in front of others on purpose, you need to stop it there and then. If you do not, that person will see you as an easy target and is likely to carry on another day. Make sure this does not become a regular occurrence. People may pretend it was a joke, that they were just messing around, but a joke can turn ugly. It may go too far, and if this happens, they may blame you while talking cynically behind your back and making you look as if you are the bad person.

Another scenario is if you are in a toxic relationship. Your self-esteem will already be low, and your partner could take advantage of this. Your partner may be an alcoholic, abusive person. But if you challenge people like this to sort out their behaviour, they may see it as a threat. They do not like being told what to do, they usually do not think rationally, and they like to control others. They usually react to situations in a bad way.

Do not forget that your mental and physical health are important here. Are you OK with this feeling of being let down all the time? Have some self-respect; remember your health is your wealth, and you deserve better than this.

Whatever situation you find yourself in right now, you need to ask yourself, *How did I get in a position like this in the first place?* Usually, the answer is that your past self was not mentally strong enough. If you cannot love and respect yourself, then what makes you think other people are going to respect you? Before they even talk to you, they will judge you by the way you dress, the way you carry yourself, the way you walk, and the way you look. Your body language tells a lot about you. And even when you talk to people, you are judged by your communication skills and by the way you speak.

So, find out where you are lacking, and then you can work on your future self. If you do not respect yourself enough or are feeling insecure around others, you need to know what the root cause is and why you have low self-esteem in the first place. Deep down, you may already know the answer, so whatever guilt-ridden thought (or any other unnecessary thought) you may have about yourself right now, you need to leave it in the past because you have held on to it for far too long. It is time for you to change that and let go of the old thinking.

So tell your old self that you forgive yourself and that you will no longer hold on to the guilt that has kept you down all these years. And when you change your thought to not having these feelings anymore (as you are now on the road to redemption), the feeling you have carried on for so long should diminish. Why hold on to guilt, as it has not done anything good for you other than making you feel bad about yourself? Time to change this for a better feeling. Why not change it for a happier one?

Exercise

Self-respect starts with you, and there are ways to get there. Take a few minutes, close your eyes, and imagine your future self staring back at you a few years into the future. Imagine what you look like and how you sound. Close your eyes and imagine now, before you read the next paragraph.

Did your future self look happy, with head held high? Is your future self a confident person? Is your future self clean, tidy, and smartly dressed? Does your future self have great communication skills? If you have mentally answered no to any of these questions, you must find out why you are not moving forward in life. Ask yourself what steps you can make to get to your future self. If you have mentally answered *yes* to any of these questions, make sure that you truthfully answered *yes*, as part 3 of this book explains the importance of never ever lying to yourself.

Here are some examples of being a better version of yourself. The clothes you are wearing can change other people's behaviour towards you. If you are wearing casual clothing on a daily basis, such as tracksuit bottoms and a regular jumper, this becomes your normal state of being. However, if you try wearing different clothing—such as a shirt, trousers, and trench coat—for at least a couple of weeks, not only will you look smart but you will feel smart also. And just by this little transformation, there will be a change in people's behaviour towards you.

You may not see this directly, but the change will be there. Just imagine seeing your future self in the mirror in a couple of months' time, looking awesome in every way. Just imagine! That could be you now.

If there is any clothing in your wardrobe you genuinely do not think suits your new self, get rid of it. Make more room for shirts, shoes, and trousers if you have to. And even changing your hairstyle can make a difference. Make it classy if you need to (if you have any hair on your head, of course). Even the way you are walking can make a difference. Walking with your head and shoulders slouched all the time can make people judge you just by that alone, and I am not joking about this; it is true. As I have said before, hold your head high.

There is an old saying that your eyes are an open window to your soul. And this is exactly it. If you start to take care of yourself more often, more good situations will come your way. If you have followed these steps with intent from this book for eating healthy and exercising regularly, you are on the road to this transition to a better self.

Remember, you have the answers to make this happen. Create an action plan for yourself to get there. It all starts with that first step.

CHAPTER 9

TRUE LIES

You may think you have never ever lied to yourself. But statistically, many people lie to themselves all the time, and they do not even realise they are doing it. Once you start telling the truth to yourself and others, there will be a fundamental shift in your conscious mind. Here are some examples where you may have lied to someone and yourself:

- **Scenario 1**

    A homeless person sitting outside a food store asks you for some spare change. Even though you are carrying lots of money, you decide to say you have none.

- **Scenario 2**

    You decide today is the day you are quitting smoking. You finish your last cigarette for the day, and then the next day, you start smoking again.

- **Scenario 3**

   You decide to start saving money, but you are spending as much as you earn.

In scenario 1, be truthful. A person may ask for some spare change. Do not lie and say "I don't have any money" if you are carrying change. Instead, tell the truth and say, "I do not have any spare change." Just because you are carrying money with you doesn't mean it is spare change. But speaking of it being spare or not, that is also a choice. You get to decide whether you want to help a person or not. But speaking the truth is a must.

In scenario 2, be truthful. If you start telling the truth to yourself, you will have a better relationship to your own mind, body, and soul. Be a person of your word. If you are not going to quit smoking, do not say it to yourself, and do not say it to others. If you do often say you are quitting but decide to continue smoking, this will make your subconscious mind weaker, as lying can become a part of your character traits. Ask yourself this simple question: where is your honesty, mainly to yourself?

In scenario 3, be truthful. When you say to yourself *I am going to start saving* but do not, you are going to be struggling constantly with money problems. The reason for this is because you already have conditioned your mind to stay in this loop. The way out of it is to make a decision (a real one) where you are creating an action plan. If you think you are not earning enough or don't have enough money to save, you need to find the root cause of that and fix it as soon as you can.

There are lots of options for you to save, such as spending smarter, changing your bill provider, and not spending money on things you do not really need. One other good way to save is to look at your finances and see where the money is being wasted unnecessarily. Be smart; do not lie yourself into debt. There a big difference between making excuses and getting the desired results.

Remember, all these scenarios are just examples. Every person's situation is different, but it all comes down to this: do not lie to yourself, and your behaviour will change for the better. If you do this consistently, you will notice a shift in your own character traits, and you will be able to do tasks with intent. You will become more in tune with your active self, your true self. One important thing is when you lie to someone else, this lie can get bigger and bigger, and when you get caught (because eventually you will get caught), you will lose credibility and trust. Others will not look at you the same way as they did before.

Other examples of when people lie to themselves include when they say they are going to make an appointment with the doctor for themselves but do not; when they say they are to going start meditating or exercising but do not; or when they say they are going to make an important phone call but do not. This way of lying to yourself has made you lazy, because you have conditioned yourself to be this way. And it is now time for you to stop that and transcend into your true self.

So speak the truth, even to yourself, and do not lie!

CHAPTER 10

CONFIDENCE

If you are an introverted individual and want good communication skills that can speak to an audience, the key is not mainly what you say but how you say it. You can improve that by listening to your own voice. Before you even get to this part, you need to stop being afraid of people staring at you. Remember your conditioned mind: you chose to be scared or shy, and you can choose not to be.

One way to overcome this is to imagine you are in a box room with a new friend, and there is no other person. There are two chairs, so you are both sitting comfortably and having a casual chat. You introduce yourself to this new friend and start talking about what school you went to, what hobbies you like, and what you do for a living. This other person does the same.

When you talk to this new friend of yours, how easy is it having a back-and-forth conversation? It is pretty easy, right? It is as easy as if you were talking to a family member or an old friend you already know. Talking to another person should come naturally, as talking is a basic human behaviour.

If you can talk to one person naturally and easily in the same room, you can do the same with two people by talking naturally and easily in the same room. All I have done is add one person. How do you feel about that now? Do you still feel the same? If so, good. If you can speak to two people naturally and easily, maybe you can speak to three people naturally and easily. And if you can speak to three people naturally and easily, you can speak to any amount of people.

You see, the key to this is that they are just numbers being added, nothing more. It is only your survival brain making this feel daunting sometimes. If you do not feel confident around an audience right now, that is because you *choose* to feel that way. But you can *choose* not to feel that way, remember, as it is always about choice and always will be.

Once you break this barrier that has held you back for so long, speaking to an audience will come naturally to you. Remember, the key theme here is that it's all about *choice*. You want to feel confident and then *choose* to be confident. You may think that you lacked confidence by autopilot and that your conditioned mind was who you were when growing up. This part maybe true, but the real truth is that you actually may have chosen this behaviour out of shyness when you were younger. The only difference is that you did not know you chose to be this way.

Your survival brain is not going to tell you this, because it does not want you to change and unlock your true potential. The good news is that you now know you can change this by choice. The next step of this section is going to be a guide for you to improve on a certain part of your confidence. It is important to carry on this exercise with intent. Become the master of your own mind.

Exercise

To improve your speech, use a recorder on your phone or any other device and start recording your own voice. Do not let your own voice put you off because that is how you sound. Yes, I understand, you do not hear your own voice every day, but once you accept your own voice, you can start to improve on your speech. Do not skip this part if you feel lazy. Choose a better, positive feeling and start practicing.

Record a small speech about anything. Make sure it lasts at least ten seconds. If you make a mistake while recording, do not stop but continue. The reason I say this is because you can pinpoint your mistake and practice this every day using different sentences. But you need continue this every day with *intent*.

When you are making a recording of your speech, make yourself sound enthusiastic all the time, because if you sound dull, your overall end results will be dull. Speak with positivity and enthusiasm, even if you have to force yourself to do so, because it is worth it. The better the results, the better your speech will get. Just keep practicing, as practice makes perfect.

Here is one speech to get you started (remember to speak with positivity/enthusiasm as you keep practicing):

> "Hello, [your name], this is your true self. I would just like to say a big thank you to you for all the past decisions that you have ever made. But it is now time for me to transform into my authentic future self."

How do you feel listening to your own recording? Do not doubt your true potential. This will be a confidence boost if you choose it to be.

Once you have tried the speech above, try any other speech that is more personal to you. Just imagine your true self now giving a speech to a wide range of audiences, and you are smiling and giving eye contact with full confidence, joy, and abundance inside you. Imagine that now.

There are also words you can change in your vocabulary to sound more professional to yourself and others. For instance, when you are speaking, use an alternate word or words in place of generic or common phrases. Let me elaborate on that. When you are agreeing or disagreeing with someone, make yourself sound superior.

For example, when you are in conversation, say *indeed* or *affirmative* instead of a generic *yes* when you are agreeing with someone. Another example is, instead of saying *let's talk about*, say *let's discuss*. These are just a few examples of the many ways you can make yourself sound better. Make your conversations sound more interesting, as people may want to listen to you more. Here are some more examples:

- Instead of *I need this*, say *I require this.*
- Instead of *I have not got this*, say *I have not received/ obtained this.*
- Instead of *We need to get more*, say *We need to generate more.*
- Instead of *We need to spend as little as possible*, say *We need to minimise our expenses.*

Practice that speech of yours before you jump to the next chapter. There are many alternative words for you to use in any conversation, such as meetings, interviews, or even casual talk. But make sure you know what you are talking about before you use some unfamiliar words, otherwise the person on the receiving end may not understand you.

Change your perception of yourself, and you'll change your outlook entirely. Energy flows where attention goes. Bring all the positive energy back inside you. Do not underestimate the true power that already resonates inside you.

PART 3

THE DECEPTION PERCEPTION

CHAPTER 11

WHAT DID YOU SEE?

If I filled up a cup of water and stopped in the middle, how would you view that? There will be two different answers: either it is half full or it is half empty. However you perceive it, the choice is yours. What you see out there is a reflection of what you see within. This is how people view information they receive.

The second example is if it is raining. Most people in England, for example, would consider it bad weather, but some people in Third World countries might consider it good weather because it helps crops to grow.

The third example is if you see someone talking to themselves out loud. You might see that individual as a mad person. But in reality, we talk to ourselves all the time. Yes, we do. The only difference is that you may not be talking out loud to yourself; but subconsciously, in your mind, you talk to yourself all the time. Every thought you have is a speech in your head before it is verbally communicated.

So, in life, you can choose what you want to be and how you see it. If you want to see good in a person, that is your choice. If you want to see bad, that is another choice. Much earlier in this book, I mentioned that dualism plays a role in your life. This has a small theme in this book, but this book is not specifically for that. I used the metaphor of your old self versus your future self as the devil and angel, if you can remember. But if you look at the foundations of dualism, it is fundamentally found everywhere.

Up, down, left, right, good, bad, right, wrong, big, small, front, back, male, female, day, night, win, lose, black, white, dead, alive, strong, weak, on, and off … I could go and on with this. The point I am trying to make is that this is a moral code/belief and resides in laws of connection, as dualism is a part of the human condition that appears everywhere. There could be a whole debate about dualism, but I am only here to explain a small part to tell you where it resides within you.

The reason I brought this up in the first place is because you have two main parts of your brain, the left hemisphere being the logical part of your mind and the right hemisphere being the creative and intuitive part. This is the point where you actually want to use both parts of your brain together, and I will help you to do this through the two exercises that follow.

Coming back to the first sentence of this chapter, what do you see in the cup of water—a cup half full or a cup half empty? Whichever way you decide to perceive it, the choice was always yours. Moving away from all this, let's do some brain exercises. This will help with your progress.

Exercise 1

There are ways to enhance your brain by exercising your mind. You can do this by using both sides of your brain at once. One way to do this is to get yourself two pens and a piece of paper. Write down the numbers from one to twenty. You have to use both hands at the same time in order to benefit from this. For example, your left hand will write down the odd numbers and your right hand will write down the even numbers. When you write down number 1 on the paper with your left hand, simultaneously, at the same time, write down number 2 on the paper with your right hand. Try it. It will feel mind-boggling at first.

Once you have done that, write the numbers 3 and 4 simultaneously. Keep carrying on all the way to 20. When you keep practicing daily, your brain capacity will strengthen. Put this book down right now and try this if you have not already. Once you have done it, only then come back to this book for the next exercise. I will see you back soon. Bye.

Have you done this exercise already? Once you have gotten used of it, you can also increase the numbers if you want to past the twentieth mark. You can even change the numbers to letters of the alphabet. Write A and B simultaneously, then go all the way to Z. Try it.

Or you can carry on with the next exercise. It's your choice. It is up to you. But I recommend that you not skip any parts, because this is benefiting *you*, not me. If you have not tried using the alphabet already, I suggest you to do so right now before you proceed to the next exercise.

Exercise 2

Start writing a sentence or paragraph with your other hand. Try this now and see how it goes. Start off with your full name, your date of birth, and your address. Then write a small description of yourself, such as where you work, how many brothers and sisters you have, and what you do for a living. Once you have done this, only then come back to read this book.

Have you done that yet?

Your handwriting may look like a toddler's. That is because you do not write with your other hand. But if you keep practicing, you will develop this skill, and it will be as good as the other hand. This is a nice skill to have, because you are enhancing yourself in more ways than you know.

This is the same as football (soccer), where most people use their right foot to kick a ball. If you are an active sports person, try to practice using your left foot when kicking a ball instead of your dominant right one. If you are already left-footed, use your right foot.

By now, you should have practiced using both sides of your brain simultaneously. How do you feel? Was it hard to do? This is just one way to enhance oneself. You will become smarter, as it will take less time for you to work things out. Just like I have used a metaphor in the previous chapters, your mind is like a computer. Current computers use solid state drives to load faster. Your mind will also work like this by thinking more quickly, efficiently, and rationally if you keep practicing the aforementioned exercise.

There are other tutorials and exercises online for you to do; you just need to search for them. Just keep practicing this as a daily routine, and not only will you enhance your mind, you will enhance your writing skills, which will be more legible when you have mastered them by yourself.

Enhance your mind and the smarter you will become.

CHAPTER 12

THE JEALOUS ONE

Moving along from brain exercises, we come to my next point. I previously discussed how other people might judge you, but how do you judge others? And how do you perceive others? Do not feel any hatred or jealousy against other people, whether friends, family, or work colleagues.

One example could be if you are at work and you have been looking for a new job for a while without any luck. Then one of your work colleagues announces that he or she has found another job or gotten a promotion. How would you feel at that moment in time? Happy for your colleague? Jealous? Would you walk up and congratulate but then deceptively hate that person? Or would you start criticising your successful colleague to others?

If you are jealous, you need to look at your own character traits and find out what you are lacking, as holding on to this feeling is only doing you harm in the long run. If you hold on to it for too long, sooner or later you are going to slip up, and the cracks are going to show your true colours to others. People are going to notice your jealousy, and they will view you as a negative character. They will judge you for who you really are. Is that who you really are? Well, it should not be.

You should not feel this way in the first place. If you feel jealous of any person, that means you are weak and comparing yourself to others. If you are comparing yourself to others, you are constantly in a bubble of fear, scanning for the next threat to your feelings of *who am I in a better position in life than*. A jealous person will usually criticise you or start comparing straight away. A person who is genuinely happy for you will usually praise you.

The moral is that no matter what status you are at, do not let your ego get the best of you. There is always going to be someone who is much richer than you or someone who is poorer than you, and that is just the way life is.

If something is beyond your control, you need to accept that and move on. Holding on to bad thoughts will only make you feel worse. Stop comparing your life to others', because it is not doing you any favours. You should treat everyone the way they would like to be treated, with respect, and then you shall be treated the same. If not, just avoid the cynics.

Remember to control your emotions. It is about choice. You get to decide how you want to feel, and you get to decide how you want to see it. Any situation you go through in life, you must see that in a neutral way. Only then can you decide which way you want to take it.

CHAPTER 13

FREEDOM AT WHAT COST?

What do you define as having freedom: having lots and lots of money? Owning a house? Whatever you choose as being free for yourself, you must try to remain your very best and not let fear take its toll on you. But you may be thinking that you do not have lots and lots of money, or maybe you do not own a house. You might be thinking, *Where does my freedom reside then, if not here?* It is all from the conditioning of your mind, because freedom comes from within. You can only be free if you truly want to be free. You may have created a prison for your own mind unintentionally.

If you do not earn much money from your wages, no matter how much money you earn, even if it is minimum wage, you need to appreciate that it is given to you. There are so many people around the world complaining that they are not earning enough, yet they do not do anything about it. And this becomes their routine, with low moods, as this can turn some of them into negative characters. They will not even know why they have become this character.

If you are working right now and are unhappy with your wages, at least appreciate it as better than having nothing at all. Do not forget that there are many people who deserve a decent wage but are jobless and desperately looking for a job. There are many who are receiving a good wage but are not deserving.

Moving on from wages and jobs, the freedom to own your own house is getting bad to worse as well. Many people cannot afford to buy a house as the housing market gets higher and higher. If you already own a mortgage-free house, good for you. Many years ago, back in my younger days, to put a deposit on a house, the agent would ask for fifty pounds. Yes, you read that right. And houses would cost on average ten thousand pounds (if you were living in the UK, of course). But do not forget that wages were also very low back then compared to what they are now. The minimum wage back then was around twenty pounds a week. And everything was cheaper as well.

The morale for an average person back then was higher than it is now because the living costs are too high in this day and age. Many years ago, the husband would go to a place of work while the wife would stay at home managing the house. The average earnings the husband made would put food on the table for the whole family. The bills would be easily paid off, and he would still have plenty of money left over. Fast forward to this present moment, and that is not possible anymore from an average wage. You need both partners to work just to get by, unless you have a great salary or are getting extra benefits from someone or something.

The point I am trying to make here is if you are a young person who wants to buy a house for the first time, it is best to be smart about it. There are many ways to make it easier. Buying a house is a serious investment. Times have changed, because trying to clear off your mortgage can take a huge chunk off your life. By the time you retire from work, you must ask yourself, *At what cost did I buy this?*

Think about it. If, for example, you are trying to buy a house which is worth a hundred and fifty thousand pounds, once you've paid it off with interest, it will be as if you have paid for three houses just to live in one. The clever banks are not going to tell you this; they are deceiving you so they can take as much money out of you as possible. If you are in a position to outsmart them, take that option.

If you start to struggle with your mortgage payments, the bank will be on your case, sending you threatening letters and emails. God forbid you do get in a financial struggle, because the bank will not care for your loss, as it is not their problem. Your house could be repossessed, and all your belongings could be taken away.

The government will not care much if you are homeless. They may pretend to be by providing you with temporary accommodation—that is, after you have already hit rock bottom. If the government was managed better, there would be no homelessness in the world. But there are too many corrupt politicians in power who are in it for themselves.

I am not here to elaborate on bankers and government. My point is, is this what freedom has cost you? You may give your house as a future investment later on to your children once you leave this world to help them have an easy future financially. But you need to ask yourself the bigger question as to why we are all in this position in the first place. This government and the world government decided to press our minds into slavery by increasing everything we buy little by little.

Think about it. If the government and world leaders decided that companies should cap the cost of everything, we would not be in this mess in the first place. Look at all the increased prices. The cost of buying food has increased, of buying clothes has increased, of buying a house has increased. Your utility bills have increased—increase after increase. When a financial collapse happens, which the government created in the first place, they look the other way and blame it on unfortunate events.

There was a survey many years back claiming that the 1960s were the best times people had; that is, because they were not bombarded by the constant rubbish of today's standards, if you know what I mean. Technology may be improving, but it is also making you weaker. One example is when people travel to a destination. They used to take a real physical map and use their brains to find out which route to take. These days, people just use GPS, and they let the GPS do the thinking for them. So tell me this: how is this helping you enhance yourself mentally?

Right now, this may seem beyond one person's control. But you still need to appreciate what you have in life and look at solutions instead of problems. Do not forget that there are many people in the world who are less fortunate than you. Many poor children in Third World countries live on the streets. This is the reason I slightly dislike these famous celebrities from Third World countries, because they are millionaires and yet they cannot even think about others and the country they live in. I understand it is their choice and they can do what they like with their money, but just think about it. They have so much money that they can wipe their own arse on it and even burn half of their fortune and still be rich.

Do not confuse me with being jealous of these people. I assure you, I am not—far from it. It is just that they have the power of money to do good deeds that can change the world to a much better one, but the majority of them turn a blind eye, mostly for selfish reasons. It is the same for world leaders. Once people get fuelled by greed, there is no stopping them.

Do not get me wrong: there are some good celebrities out there who are trying to help by being philanthropists, but only to a certain extent. What would happen if all the world's millionaires came together in one place and decided to use this wealth to point us in a positive direction—a direction in which the people of the world actually *cared* for each other, in which we wiped out poverty forever, in which everyone got a proper education. This is my wishful thinking, but it can happen if the people in power choose. Yet they choose not to.

Success does not start with other people; it starts with you. You may get help from other people or tools to get you there, but you have to decide whether it's the right thing to do or the wrong thing. So choose wisely!

CHAPTER 14

YOU BELIEVE IN WHAT?

If I sat you down and had a serious discussion about whether or not you believe in Santa Claus, you immediately would think I was absurd. OK, I can understand. You can say these things to children, because it gives them the excitement of looking forward to Christmas, but I cannot get my head around why some adults believe in fairy tales. And I am not thinking about Santa Claus. The fairy tales I am thinking about are how many adults around the world believe in superstitious beliefs. I am not referring to angels and demons here or any other supernatural belief. If you want to believe this, that is your choice. I am thinking of superstitious beliefs that have no real impact on you and others, as you will come to read in a moment.

These superstitious beliefs are created through fear and are passed on from generation to generation. These nonsense beliefs have no real impact on your life. Once you realise this, you can overcome these absurd thoughts. This will have a profound effect on your life, as you will no longer have the need to feel anxious or worried by believing you are going to get bad luck just because you did something or saw something.

You may have trusted these absurd beliefs because when you were younger, people around you repeated the same nonsense they heard from other people when they were growing up. Then adults even tell their children, and children tell their friends. This has a cause-and-effect in your subconscious mind, as people are conditioning each other with this nonsense information. You may hear this from all walks of life.

Let's have a look at some examples of these absurd beliefs. In England, if you see a magpie, you get bad luck. You smash a mirror, you get bad luck. You walk under a ladder, you get bad luck. You cross paths with somebody in the stairs, you get bad luck. There are too many to count, because the bad luck you create for yourself differs from country to country. I know, it is mind-boggling to even think that so many people around the world have decided to believe in such nonsense that it is stopping them from becoming their true authentic self.

If people have a very superstitious mind, they will limit their own possibilities, because if anything bad happens, they will automatically blame the situation they believe has caused it. One example is if people accidentally breaks a mirror. They are going to think they are going to have so many years of bad luck, and if anything bad does happen in the aftermath, such as they get a flat tyre on their car, they are going to automatically relate that to the broken mirror, even though it had nothing to do with it. Free your mind from these beliefs, I recommend.

Remember, these kinds of beliefs are holding you back in life. Once you let them go, and only when you let them go, you can start to transform into a better version of yourself, just like a butterfly transforming from a cocoon. Get out of your cocoon and fly. Break free from the shackles of your old self, as this old belief system needs to go. All these beliefs are man-made. Do not become the fool; become your true self instead.

These fairly-tale beliefs have kept you in a box. It is time for you to step out of it and perceive reality for what it really is.

PART 4

SPIRITUALITY

CHAPTER 15

CONNECTIONS AND DISCONNECTIONS

Whether you believe in religion or are an atheist, that is your business. This section of this book can be controversial to some people. I am not attacking anyone's beliefs. But I do have to say this: If you are a religious person, then your religion is the best. Yes—yours and nobody else's. Your religion is the right path and others are wrong. Now if you really believe this statement, how wrong you are.

You need to know that all religions are man-made. All of them. God did not create religion; people did. People believe using religion will get them closer to God by praying their sins away and going to their place of worship regularly.

It is ironic that some people born into their race or religion point to their own god(s), or themselves, as being the superior religion or race. Imagine yourself being born in a different race or religion from the one you are in now. You might think that this is nonsense, but just try to visualise that. If you cannot, you have a mind closed to new information. You are holding on to your limited beliefs.

I am not asking you to change religions. I would never try to convert anyone. The reason I am saying to think out of the box is because if you was born in a different race or religion other than the one you are now, your views and beliefs about that specific religion or race would be very different.

In truth, religions have separated people and disconnected us, because each religion wants you to behave and think in a certain way which slightly differs from other religions. That is why the world is the way it is. Imagine if we were all more spiritual with ourselves and each other. We could turn this world into a haven if we wanted to. But this will never happen, due to so many negative people having cynical views about other people in this world.

Speaking of religion, it is making you go further away from God. The reason for this is if people says they are men and women of peace, but because of their egos they start attacking other people (mentally or physically) because those on the receiving end have a different belief system, what does this show you about the people of peace? They are mostly hypocritical and narrow-minded. They only believe what is true in their own mind, and every other religion is unnecessary to them.

Some people may label me a blasphemer. But the truth is, I am far from it. I believe in God in a spiritual way, but I do not bring all the religious baggage that comes with it, because God is everywhere, right? And who ever portrayed god as a male figure? We did. God is never in human form. Do not be fooled by films or any other concept portraying God as human.

There was a great philosopher who said, "Before we label ourselves of what religion we are, let us be civilised first." That is true—we all need to be civilised before we label ourselves as to what religion we claim to be. The problem is that a few too many religious people cannot do that because they use religion as an excuse to look down on other people. If you do not believe what they believe, they may label you as a person of low status (a peasant) in their eyes.

I am not saying that every religious person will think this way, but we all have met at least one fanatic who does. In truth, it does not matter what you look like, what ethnicity you are, or what nation you were born in. You are not superior to anyone, and they are not superior to you. We all come from the same source of infinite consciousness—that is, from the mysteries of spirituality.

When you label yourself as a certain religion, you may be not properly civilised to your true self as you start viewing and judging other people differently because their religion is not the same as yours. Imagine, for example, that you lived in an alternate world where there was no religion and even no races. The only way you could ever judge people is by their deeds and actions, not their religion and race. We would be more civilised if this really happened.

But this wishful thinking. It is never going to happen, because too many people are disconnected, and most people are out for themselves. Selfish motives disconnect us.

Spirituality connects us, and religion does not. You may disagree with this statement. That is up to you. But honestly, tell the truth to yourself. When was the last time you saw a religious person go to a different place of worship other than the one his or her religion is based upon and pray there? It is a very rare sight indeed. This is how are divided.

And this is where spirituality comes in. We are all spiritually connected to each other, but at the same time, we are all mentally disconnected. This is due to having different beliefs. Spiritual people see other individuals as one, and they will not attack or harm anyone physically or mentally, regardless of what that individual looks like or does. They believe that if you attack someone mentally or physically, spiritually you are attacking yourself. That is how a real spiritualist thinks. A spiritualist know the importance of life.

There are so many corrupt people in this world—scammers, deranged hackers, drug dealers, the list goes on and on. They come from all walks of life. These human parasites are everywhere, trying to distress good people. This is the other challenge we must face together as a world, and not by looking the other way. This can make good people lose faith in humanity.

If good people hold on to each other and do at least one good deed a day, there will always be hope. The good will always triumph over evil, even though we may not see it. Karma will always bite back eventually. In the next chapter, we will go even deeper into spirituality.

To be one with God, you only need to speak through spirituality.

CHAPTER 16

OUR WORLD, OUR SICKNESS

We are a part of this Mother Earth. This is our home, your home. Yet there are so many people across all walks of life treating their home planet as garbage. It is these kinds of bad habits, like throwing litter on the ground or putting out too much emissions, that are making the earth deteriorate slowly over time. And this Earth is not like it used to be, as it was once a land of enormous beauty and paradise.

To understand how you are spiritually connected to Mother Earth, consider this metaphor: If you examined the blood in your body with a powerful telescope, you would notice that each cell in your body is in an active state. You would see that you have millions and millions of cells. Whether you care or do not care, most of these cells are working in your favour, although some are working against you.

Now imagine zooming out of Earth itself so you are looking at the solar system. Imagine Mother Earth as a human being just like yourself who is living life as it should be, and we humans are the millions and millions of cells traveling around her body. Whether we care or do not care, there are cells (humans) who wants to damage the planet and cells (humans) who want to save it. My question to you is, which side of evolution are you on right now?

As a human gets sick, the planet can also get sick. How does this planet get sick, you may ask? By having all sorts of viruses and pollution in the world. It is all about the cleanliness of the earth. Our past generations have taken this in a wrong direction, and we are the ones picking up where they left off.

One example from our past generations taking things in a wrong direction is so many people smoking cancer sticks such as cigarettes and cigars. Even today, there are so many people smoking in the world right now. And what is all this smoke doing to the earth right now? Well, I will give a clue: it is not doing the earth any good, is it?

Imagine an alternate world where no one smoked and no one had ever heard of smoking (if our ancestors took it in this direction, of course). You are now the only person on planet Earth who smokes. When you have a cigarette, people look at you in shock. What do you believe they are thinking of you? They may think that you have an illness, and the cigarette you keep puffing on is your medication.

I understand that people may need medicine when they feel ill, but a cigarette is not a medicine to make you feel better. It is a drug for your mind that will keep you hooked on it because of the addictive nicotine. So if you are a cigarette smoker and are trying to quit, my question to you is, "Do you have an illness because you cannot quit smoking?" If you say, "No, I do not have an illness," then prove it. Prove it to me now by throwing those cigarette packets away and never touching them again, as they are not needed in your life. They never were.

Remember to think with intent. Do not be offended by what I have stated just now. I am only trying to make you understand that it is actually easy for you to quit. It's not hard at all—only your survival brain makes you think that it is hard. Prove your old self wrong.

But back to speaking about planet Earth, I would just like to address that there are many other events or situations that are damaging this planet. It is your duty to treat this planet right. Even a small change like spitting gum in the bin instead of on the sidewalk makes a difference, yet there are so many people around the world who do not do this, as they have conditioned themselves to be ignorant.

Remember, you are a fundamental part of this Earth, and this Earth is a part of you. Take more care of it, because this is your home and always has been. We all come from the same infinite consciousness.

CHAPTER 17

DETACHMENT FROM EVERYTHING

If you are not a vegetarian and call yourself a spiritual person, maybe you need to rethink that. Spiritualists see all living things on earth as God's creatures, whether human or animal. If you decide one day that you are going to turn vegetarian, making the transition is not as difficult as you may think. The change can happen in an instant. By now, you should know the secret to changing this behaviour of yours. I am not here to convince you to turn into a vegetarian. That is, of course, your choice—if you want to change, that is.

This is the same as any other craving you might have. You just have to detach your mind from the attachment by choice. But it doesn't stop there, as there are so many things you are attached to right now, such as places, people, or items. I am not saying this is a bad thing; what I am saying is that if you are too attached to someone or something, bringing so many of your emotions with you, it is only going to hurt you more in the long run if something bad happens.

For instance, if you are in a good relationship with your partner and suddenly your partner decides to leave you, you may now perceive that person in a more hateful way. But deep down, that person hasn't changed. You are just reacting differently now. This unfortunate event can hurt you so much because you have conditioned yourself to think this way, as you still may be in your comfort zone. This can lead to depression if you are not careful, as you may not be using your mind correctly. In order to not to be in this position in the first place, you have to control your emotions by being proactive with your thought patterns. You need to think as neutral as possible every day, the stoic way.

There is no good; there is no bad. A problem only becomes a problem if you want it to be one. Regardless of any situation and obstacle you may encounter on a day-to-day basis, you have to think like a stoic; that will help you be stronger mentally and calmer under pressure.

I am not saying you cannot have these feelings for someone or have these feelings of pressure, but when the time comes, you need to be prepared to outwit your old self, as your old self might get the better of you. Once you have mastered a stoic mind, you will be able to handle any situation efficiently.

Another example to detach your mind is, if you are spending too much time on technology such as phones or laptops. You can test yourself now. Can you leave your phone at home while you are at work for at least one week? If you cannot leave your phone at home even for a couple of days, you are too attached to your phone. Remember what the main functionalities are for a phone: to ring for emergencies. But phone companies have manipulated your way of thinking to keep you addicted by making them smart. The only smart part is the companies who have you trapped in technology. Do not take this the wrong way—they are good as a tool when needed, but so many people are overusing their phone unnecessarily. They have become so attached to it that it's taking over their life.

You may think, *If I do not have this, I will get bore*d. I want to share my own thoughts about this. I very rarely get bored because I have conditioned myself not to think this way by choice, even if I am not doing anything. You can do the same; you just need to know how to detach yourself from yourself. Know your true self, and it will set you free from unnecessary thoughts such as boredom. And you will never feel bored again.

All you need to do is master your mind. You know how to do this now. Only you can do this; I cannot do it for you. I can only show you the way. Remember, it is mind control.

Control your mind before it controls you. Do not be someone who needs constant technology just to get through your daily routine. Are you watching random videos every day? People watch these for entertainment purposes. If you are watching them because you have nothing else to do, this has become an unnecessary habit.

Ask yourself this question: *What other ways can I make myself preoccupied without too much use of technology in my spare time?* Do not be trapped in this loop by your survival brain of having to spend all your spare time on unnecessary situations. Take that spare time to a more meaningful direction, because when you look back in life, you will ask yourself, *Why did I not pursue this?* or *I could have achieved something that had good value.*

And speaking of adding more value to your life, you deserve better than this right now. You deserve more than just your old way of thinking. I know you have good intentions, and these can go a long way in a more meaningful direction, more than you may ever know.

Your mind can have thoughts of infinite possibilities. Do not narrow your mind by conditioning yourself to think small and only in one direction, as once you do that, your survival brain will make it harder for you to think above and beyond to what you are truly capable of. Right now, you are more capable of being your true self than you know. You just have to unlock the secret door hidden in your mind to new empowering information that will take you to your true authentic self. If you have already followed this guide thoroughly, you should be already on your way.

And there is more to life than this. Imagine yourself many years in the future and feel proud of what good things and good deeds you have done for yourself, people, places, and Earth itself. In order for you to get there, you need to keep doing good deeds, as you must put your thoughts into action and start moving forward. You are more than just getting up in the morning, going to work, going to sleep, and repeating. If you are not currently happy right now, use the techniques provided in this book, because feeling unhappy is not the real you.

The most prominent role while being your true self is carrying on this journey with your passion and intent, as there is no end goal for continuous self-improvement. Leave a legacy behind that you feel proud of, not for your own ego but for life in general. One other thing is you cannot take all your possessions with you when your time is over. We are here on a temporary basis called life, and it is your duty to be your best.

Do not be stranded in old thought. Think like a stoic!

FROM THE TIES THAT BIND US

In conclusion, you may be thinking, *Where do I go next on my life journey?* The answer is easy: you just have to keep putting one foot in front of the other, and as I have said before, just keep moving forward and do not look back, as your past has very little use for you now. Each new day is a test for you to become a better version of yourself.

You may think, *How can I improve myself to become more than I already am?* The answer to that is, do not become your old self again, as it is will always be at the back end of your subconscious mind. It is your duty to keep it from popping up again.

You must keep reminding yourself every day that you can *choose* how you want to behave, how you want to react, how you want to feel, and how you want others to view you in any situation in your life. This is done by controlling your thinking about what you say, your body language, and even your dress code. Remember, you can only do your best, and you cannot please everyone. That is the way life is. The way your thoughts were conditioned at an early age can be changed by choice.

How you communicate is also important to your success. But what is success really? Success could mean anything. If you are a happy person in general, that is success. If you achieve a personal goal, that is success. If you have mastered your mind, that is also success. Let yourself become a success story. What you have learnt from this book, should give you an advantage in whatever you are trying to achieve, and you do not need to be compared to anyone except your old self. Do not turn your thoughts into a competition if they are not one.

Start looking after your health more often because nothing is better than what nature has given you. If you know your health is deteriorating and you are going to do nothing about it, do not hate yourself by punishing yourself, as this is making it worse. Stop feeling sorry for yourself, because you are the one who is going to suffer physically or mentally in the long run, no one else. It is your responsibility to do the right thing.

Open your mind to new thoughts and information. Holding on to old thoughts all these years has kept you in a bubble. I have faith that you will be a happier person if you use your mind the way I have told you. But this transition from your old self to your new self depends on how you want to get there.

Now that you are at the end of this book, my question to you is, did you try the techniques I presented? If you have understood correctly and read each chapter with intent, as I have told you, the rewiring of your thoughts will already have been noticed by your true self. Do not lie to yourself or others, as you will have a better relationship not only with your true self but with others as well.

All I will say to you is, carry on with your journey with a strong healthy mind, because obstacles will come at you at any time, and your old self may come back again. Do not let your old self come back. You can turn any problem you face in life into a solution easily. How? A problem will only be a problem if you want to view it as a problem. It is about changing your perspective and dealing with it in a better and more efficient way. The power is already inside you. Unlock your true self and become free from worry, stress, anxiety, and other nonessential thinking that does not serve your best interest.

There is an old anonymous Japanese quote which says:

> You have three faces.
> The first face you show the world.
> The second face you show your close friends
>   and family.
> The third face you never show anyone, and
>   this third face is the truest reflection of
>   who you are.

But this is not who you are anymore. This was your old self. Your true self will only show one face and will not need to hide any insecurities or secrets from people, as you do not need to because you should not have any—well, not anymore. And your authentic self is the truest reflection of who you are. You will not only show this to the world, your friends, and your family, you will also show your old self that it has been beaten and you have mastered self-thought.

One last thing I would like to say is that happiness is also a key part to your success. Do not think and say everybody knows this, because if this was the case, you would already be following through. So search for what makes you happy. Do not assume that people with lots of money are happy, because I have seen a few too many who either have lots of it and become anxious about losing it all or have other psychological issues, such as becoming so greedy it makes them egoistic. Do not let this be you. Know how to be responsible with your money; otherwise, it will control you.

Do not put all your happiness on money alone. Remember, money is just a survival tool—but if you need more of it, there are plenty of ways to get it. Even a poor person can be happier than a rich one. What is the point of having too much money if deep inside you are unhappy with life? Happiness is within you, so change your conditioning, and you will change your end result. Just remember: if you do have low self-esteem, you have the power to turn your thoughts positive again, and you now know what skill is required to do so.

Here is my last question for you: who is doing your real thinking now: your old self or the real you? Be one with your new self, your authentic self, and not with the bogus one. From here on out, you will know what to do in order to get the best version of yourself in any situation. If you ever have the desire to read this book again, do it.

This is the end, where I will leave you and love you unconditionally, as this is just the beginning of your true identity. The journey does not end with this book. This wisdom will always be with you, as it is all in your subconscious mind. You just have keep showing up every day by being the one and only true version of yourself. Do not let the old self creep back in. Remember, it is not you versus the world but rather you versus yourself.

Free your mind from your old self. Everything is connected within all of us. These are the ties that bind us all together. We are all one big family spiritually and always were. Do not forget that.

If you found this book useful in any way, please feel free to help others by telling them about it, as this small gesture goes a long way. I would like to say a big thank-you to you, because you have finished reading this whole book with integrity. Goodbye for now, authentic reader! And may you have a great journey as your true self.

Printed in the United States
by Baker & Taylor Publisher Services